JOURNEYS
COMMON CORE

Program Authors

James F. Baumann · David J. Chard · Jamal Cooks · J. David Cooper · Russell Gersten · Marjorie Lipson
Lesley Mandel Morrow · John J. Pikulski · Héctor H. Rivera · Mabel Rivera · Shane Templeton · Sheila W. Valencia
Catherine Valentino · MaryEllen Vogt

Consulting Author
Irene Fountas

Cover illustration by Scott Nash.

Printed in the U.S.A.

ISBN 978-0-547-91230-1

6 7 8 9 10 0868 21 20 19 18 17 16 15 14 13

4500414983   A B C D E F G

Unit 1

Unit 2

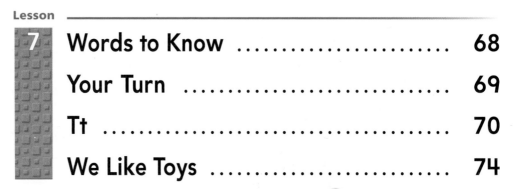

Unit 3

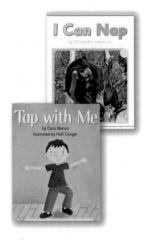

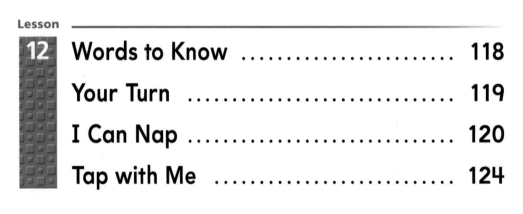
6

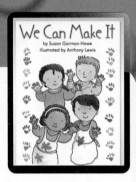

See What We Can Do
by Susan Gorman-Howe
illustrated by Sue Dennen

We Can Make It
by Susan Gorman-Howe
illustrated by Anthony Lewis

✓ **WORDS TO KNOW**
High-Frequency Words

I

Vocabulary Reader

Sisters and Brothers

Context Cards

I have a big family!

COMMON CORE
RI.K.1 ask and answer questions about key details; **RF.K.3c** read common high-frequency words by sight; **SL.K.2** confirm understanding of a text read aloud or information presented orally or through other media by asking/answering questions and requesting clarification

Go Digital

Words to Know

Read Together

▸ Read the word.

▸ Talk about the picture.

I

I have a big family!

Your Turn

Talk About It!

What Makes a Family?

by Pam Muñoz Ryan

Families are different. What is the same about all families? Share ideas with a partner.

See What We Can Do

by Susan Gorman-Howe

illustrated by Sue Dennen

We Can Make It

by Susan Gorman-Howe

illustrated by Anthony Lewis

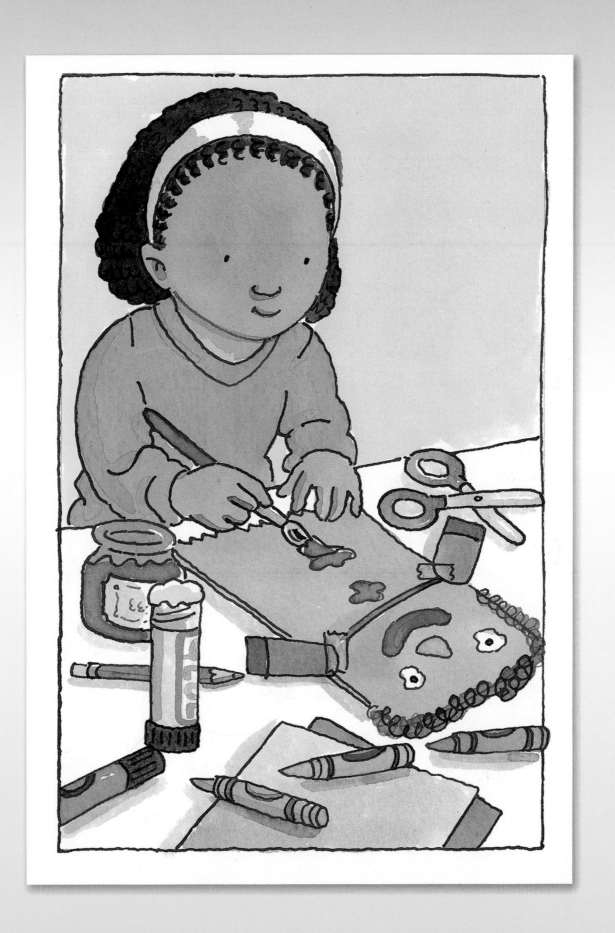

Words to Know

Read Together

☑ **WORDS TO KNOW**
High-Frequency Words

like

Vocabulary Reader

Context Cards

COMMON CORE **RL.K.1** ask and answer questions about key details; **RF.K.3c** read common high-frequency words by sight; **SL.K.2** confirm understanding of a text read aloud or information presented orally or through other media by asking/answering questions and requesting clarification

▶ Read the word.

▶ Talk about the picture.

like

We like to go to school!

Your Turn

Talk About It!

Why do we have rules at school? Talk about it with a friend.

We Go to School

by Susan Gorman-Howe

illustrated by Maryann Cocca-Leffler

I Like

by Owen Marcus

illustrated by Maribel Suarez

I like .

I like .

I like .

I like  .

Words to Know

Read Together

Baby Bear's Family
by Susan Gorman-Howe
illustrated by Angela Jarecki

The Party
by Ron Kingsley
illustrated by Yvette Banek

✓ **WORDS TO KNOW**
High-Frequency Words

the

Vocabulary Reader

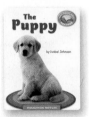
The Puppy
by Isabel Johnson

Context Cards

Do you see the puppy?

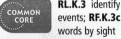
COMMON CORE **RL.K.3** identify characters, settings, and major events; **RF.K.3c** read common high-frequency words by sight

Go Digital

▸ Read the word.

▸ Talk about the picture.

the

1

Do you see **the** puppy?

Your Turn

Talk About It!

Talk to a friend. Tell why pets need someone to take care of them.

Baby Bear's Family

by Susan Gorman-Howe

illustrated by Angela Jarecki

The Party

by Ron Kingsley

illustrated by Yvette Banek

I like the .

I like the .

I like the .

I like the .

and

Vocabulary Reader

Context Cards

Words to Know

Read Together

▸ Read the word.

▸ Talk about the picture.

and

A worker has a saw and a hammer.

Your Turn

Everybody Works

Talk About It!

What kinds of work do people do? Tell a partner.

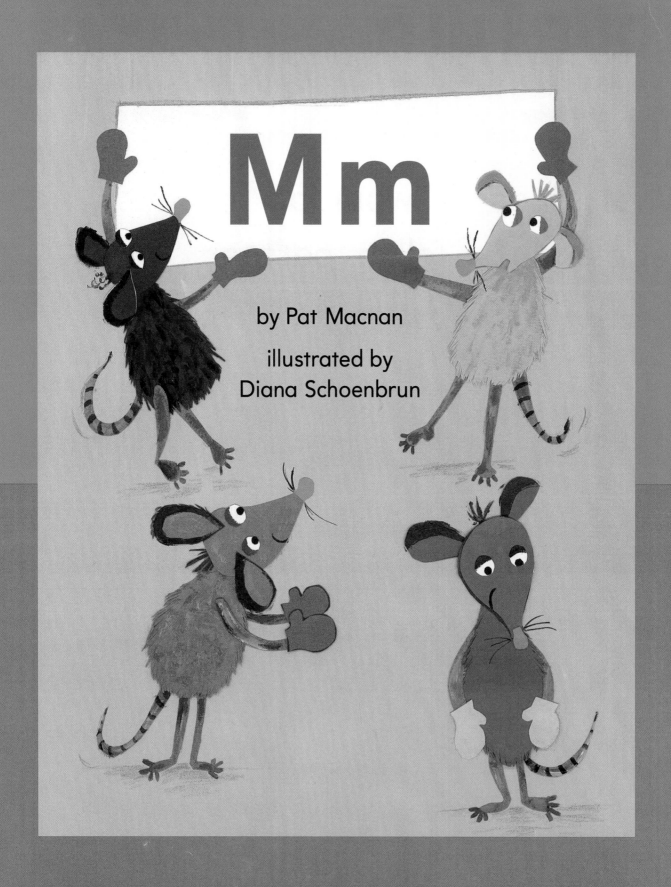

Mm

by Pat Macnan

illustrated by
Diana Schoenbrun

Mm

I Like Mm

by Pat Macnan

I like the .

Mm

I like the  .

I like the .

Mm

I like the 🥛 and the 🧁🧁.

✓ **WORDS TO KNOW**
High-Frequency Words

I
like

Vocabulary Reader

Context Cards

COMMON CORE **RI.K.7** describe relationships between illustrations and the text; **RF.K.3c** read common high-frequency words by sight

Go Digital

Words to Know

Read Together

▶ You learned these words. Use each one in a sentence.

I

I have a big family!

like

We like to go to school!

Your Turn

Talk About It!

The Handiest Things
in the World
ANDREW CLEMENTS
Photographs by Raquel Jaramillo

How do tools help us do
things with our hands?
Tell a partner what you think.

Ss

by Pat Macnan

illustrated by Diana Schoenbrun

I Like Ss

by Pablo Lopez

I like the 🛥️.

I like the .

I like the ☀.

Ss

I like the  and the .

☑ **WORDS TO KNOW**
High-Frequency Words

see

Vocabulary Reader

Look at Me!
by Olivia Rose
illustrated by Marilyn Janovitz

Context Cards

RI.K.1 ask and answer questions about key details; **RF.K.3c** read common high-frequency words by sight

Go Digital

Words to Know
Read Together

▶ Read the word.

▶ Talk about the picture.

see

What can you **see** in the city?

Your Turn

Talk About It!

How do you use your senses to learn about the world? Tell a friend.

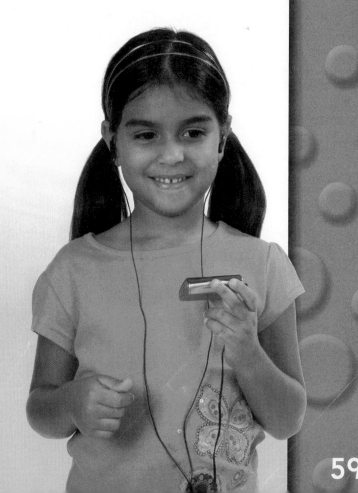

Aa

by Roberto Livingston
illustrated by Bernard Adnet

Aa

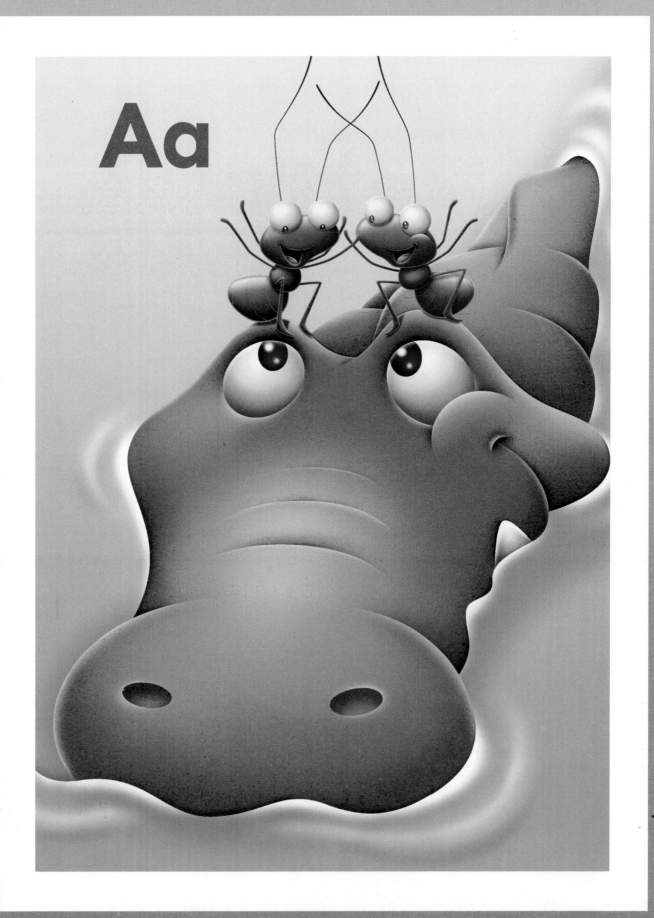

I See

by Sheila Hoffman

I see the .

Aa

I see the .

Aa

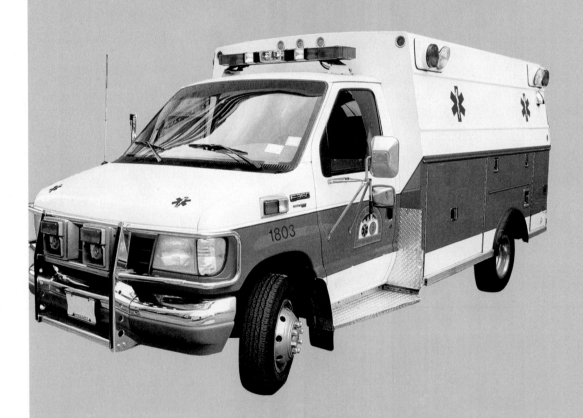

I see the .

Aa

I see the 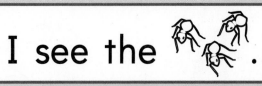.

Tt
by Nimesh Sing
illustrated by Priscilla Burris

We Like Toys
by Matthew Lorer

✓ **WORDS TO KNOW**
High-Frequency Words

we

Vocabulary Reader

On the Farm
by Alex Carro

Context Cards

Our cat purrs when we pet her.

COMMON CORE **RL.K.1** ask and answer questions about key details; **RF.K.3c** read common high-frequency words by sight

Go Digital

Words to Know

Read Together

▸ Read the word.

▸ Talk about the picture.

we

Our cat purrs when we pet her.

Your Turn

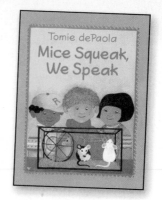

Talk About It!

How do people and animals communicate? Talk about it with a friend. Use words from the **Big Book** as you share ideas.

Tt

by Nimesh Sing

illustrated by Priscilla Burris

Tt

Tt

73

We Like Toys

by Matthew Lorer

Tt

I like the .

Tt

We like the 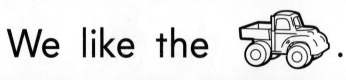.

Tt

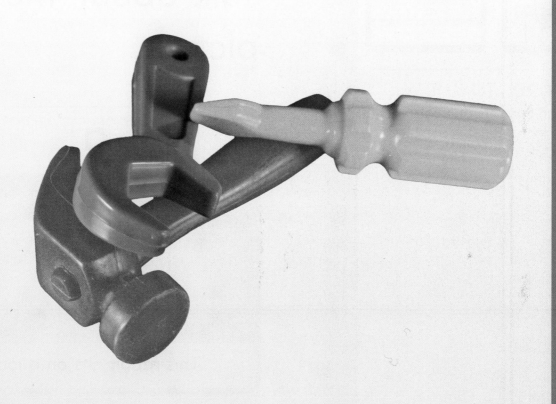

We like the 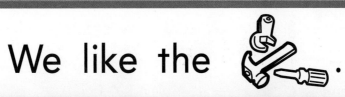.

8

I Can See

✓ **WORDS TO KNOW**
High-Frequency Words

a

Vocabulary Reader

Context Cards

Visiting a Park
by Sarah Schneider

This rabbit sits on a log.

COMMON CORE

RI.K.1 ask and answer questions about key details; **RI.K.7** describe relationships between illustrations and the text; **RF.K.3c** read common high-frequency words by sight

Go Digital

Words to Know

Read Together

▸ Read the word.

▸ Talk about the picture.

a

1

This rabbit sits on a log.

Your Turn

Talk About It!

Why do different animals move in different ways? Talk about it with a friend.

Cc

by David Ashford

illustrated by John Segal

Cc

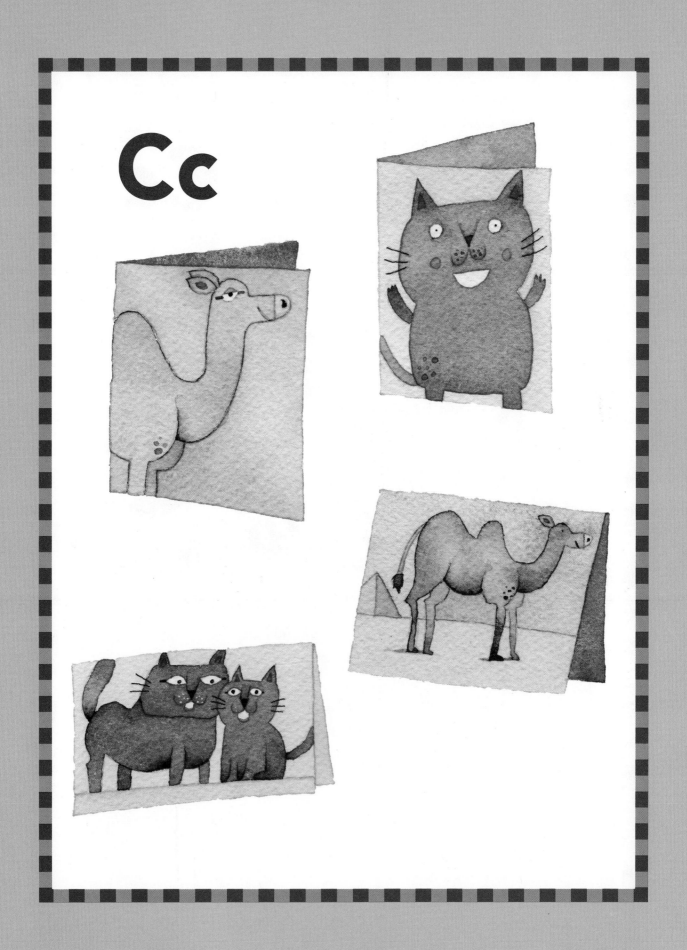

I Can See

by Laticia Craven

I see a 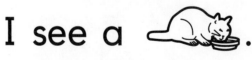.

Cc

I see a .

Cc

I see a 💻 .

Cc

I see a  .

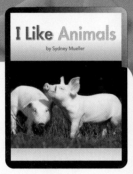

✓ **WORDS TO KNOW**
High-Frequency Words

to

Vocabulary Reader

Context Cards

COMMON CORE **RI.K.7** describe the relationship between illustrations and the text; **SL.K.2** confirm understanding of a text read aloud or information presented orally or through other media by asking/answering questions and requesting clarification; **RF.K.3c** read common high-frequency words by sight

Words to Know

Read Together

▸ Read the word.

▸ Talk about the picture.

to

We like **to** ride our bikes!

Your Turn

Talk About It!

Why do people use wheels?
Talk with a partner.

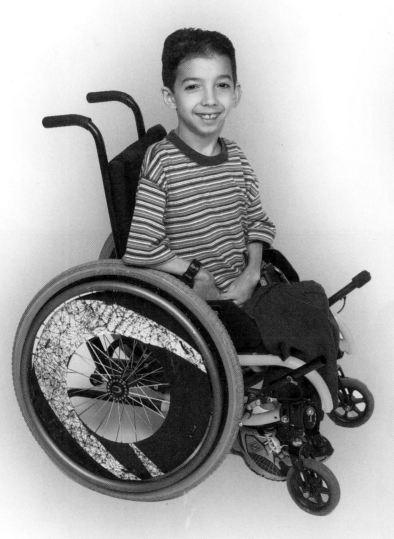

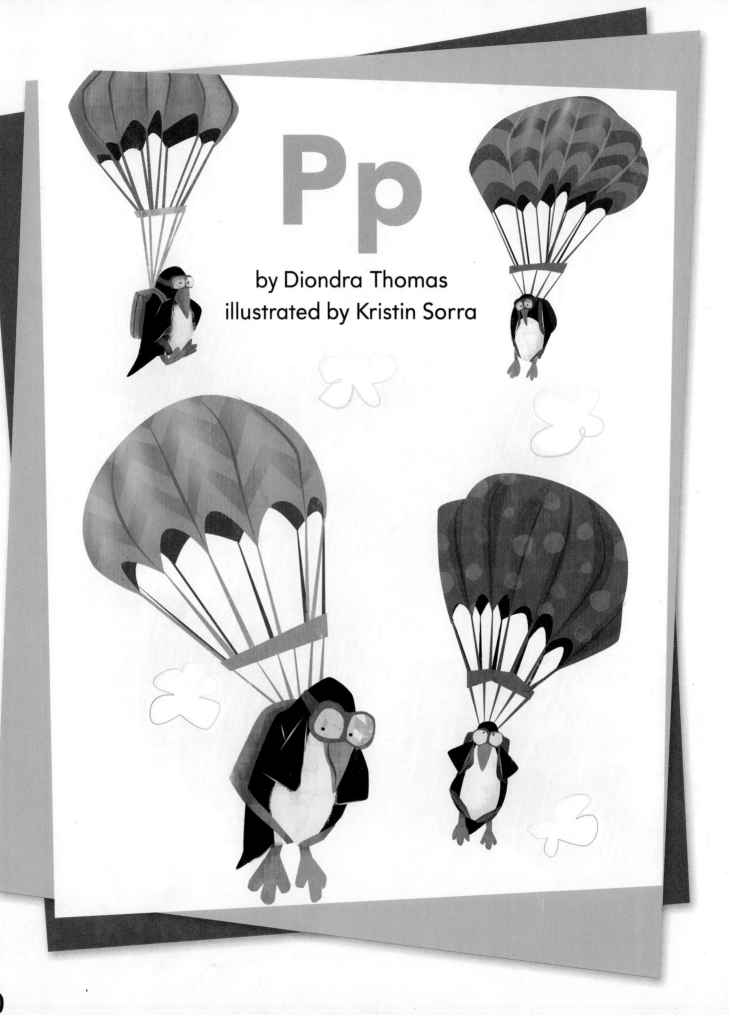

P p

by Diondra Thomas
illustrated by Kristin Sorra

Pp

I Like Animals

by Sydney Mueller

I like to see .

Pp

I like to see .

Pp

I like to see 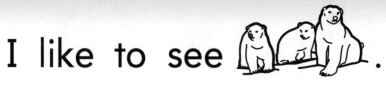 .

Pp

I like to see .

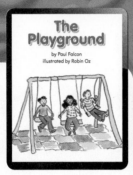

Mmmm, Good!
by Angela Ferie
illustrated Ana Ochoa

The Playground
by Paul Falcon
illustrated by Robin Oz

✓ **WORDS TO KNOW**
High-Frequency Words

see

we

Vocabulary Reader

Context Cards

COMMON CORE **RL.K.1** ask and answer questions about key details; **RL.K.3** identify characters, settings, and major events; **RF.K.3c** read common high-frequency words by sight

Go Digital

Words Read Together to Know

▶ You learned these words. Use each one in a sentence.

see

What can you see in the city?

we

Our cat purrs when we pet her.

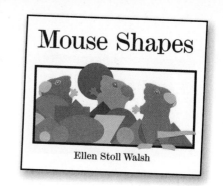

Your Turn

Talk About It!

What can we create with shapes? Talk with a partner.

Mmmm, Good!

by Angela Ferie
illustrated Ana Ochoa

I see .

I like .

We like  .

We like to see .

The Playground

by Paul Falcon

illustrated by Robin Oz

I like the .

I like to  .

We see the  .

We like the .

Come and See Me
by Greg Kent

Pam and Me
by Louise Andreas
illustrated by Judith Lanfredi

✓ **WORDS TO KNOW**
High-Frequency Words

come

me

Vocabulary
Reader

Context
Cards

Fun in July
by Zachary Landau

The rain will come down in spring.

COMMON CORE

RI.K.1 ask and answer questions about key details; **RI.K.10** engage in group reading activities with purpose and understanding; **RF.K.3c** read common high-frequency words by sight

Go Digital

Words **Read Together**
to Know

▸ Read the words.

▸ Talk about the pictures.

come

The rain will come down in spring.

me

This hat is for me.

Your Turn

Talk About It!

How does the weather change in different months and seasons? Talk to a friend about it.

Come and See Me

by Greg Kent

Pat Cat, Pat Cat!

Pat, Pat, Pat!

Come to me, Pat Cat!
Pat Cat sat.

Sam Cat, Sam Cat!
Sam, Sam, Sam!

Come to me, Sam Cat!
Sam Cat sat.

Pam and Me

by Louise Andreas

illustrated by Judith Lanfredi

Pam, Pam, Pam, Pam!

Pam, Pam, Pam.
Come to me, Pam.

I sat. Pam Cat sat.

I pat Pam.
Pat, pat, pat.

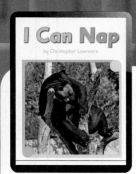
I Can Nap
by Christopher Lawrence

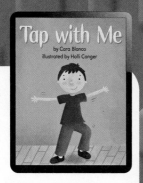
Tap with Me
by Cara Blanca
illustrated by Holli Conger

☑ **WORDS TO KNOW**
High-Frequency Words

with

my

Vocabulary Reader

Context Cards

Animals in the Snow

COMMON CORE **RL.K.1** ask and answer questions about key details; **RF.K.3c** read common high-frequency words by sight

Go Digital

Words to Know

Read Together

▶ Read the words.

▶ Talk about the pictures.

with

1

The trees are covered with snow.

my

2

The snowman wears my scarf.

Your Turn

Talk About It!

snow

Manya Stojic

What do animals do when the weather changes? Talk to a partner about it.

I Can Nap

by Christopher Lawrence

 can nap.
Nap, nap, nap, nap.

I can nap with my .
Nap, nap, nap, nap.

 can nap.

Nap, nap, nap, nap.

I can nap with my .
Nap, nap, nap, nap.

Tap with Me

by Cara Blanco

illustrated by Holli Conger

I can tap.

I tap, tap, tap.

I can tap. Nan can tap.
Nan can tap, tap, tap.

I can tap with Nan.
Tap, tap, tap.

I am Tap Man!
Tap, tap, tap! Tap Man!

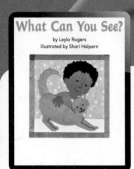
What Can You See?
by Leyla Rogers
illustrated by Shari Halpern

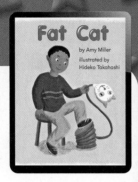
Fat Cat
by Amy Miller
illustrated by Hideko Takahashi

✓ **WORDS TO KNOW**
High-Frequency Words

you

what

Vocabulary Reader

Lots of Birds

Context Cards

Do you see the butterfly?

COMMON CORE **RI.K.1** ask and answer questions about key details; **RF.K.3c** read common high-frequency words by sight; **SL.K.1a** follow rules for discussions

Go Digital

Words to Know

Read Together

▸ Read the words.

▸ Talk about the pictures.

you

1

Do you see the butterfly?

what

2

What colors do you see?

Your Turn

Talk About It!

What Do You Do With a Tail Like This?
Steve Jenkins & Robin Page

How do animals use their body parts? Talk to a partner about it.

What Can You See?

by Leyla Rogers
illustrated by Shari Halpern

Cam can see a tan cat.
A tan, tan, tan cat!
Cam can see a fat tan cat.

Fan can see Nat.
Can Nat see Fan?
Nat can! Nat can!

Pam can see Sam nap.
Nap, nap, nap, Sam!

Can Mac see you?

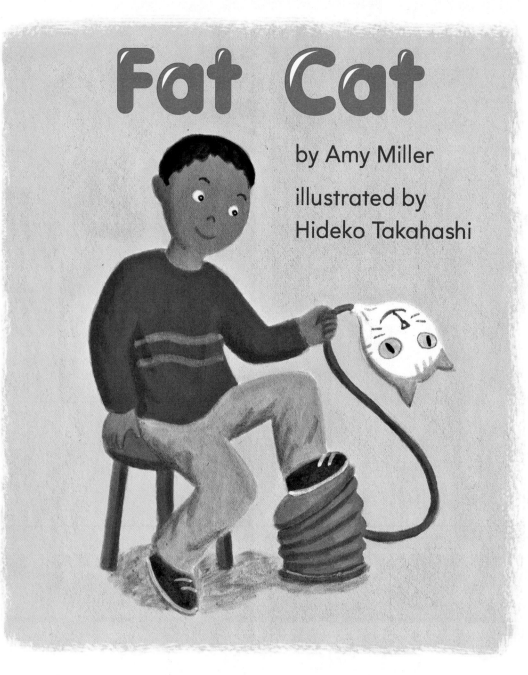

Fat Cat

by Amy Miller

illustrated by
Hideko Takahashi

Can you see Sam?
Sam can tap, tap, tap.

Tap, Sam, tap.
Tap, tap, tap, Sam.

Tap, Sam!
Tap. Tap. Tap.

Can you see the fat cat?
What a fat, fat, fat cat!

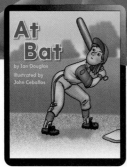

What Now?
by Suzanne Gerardi

At Bat
by Ian Douglas
illustrated by
John Ceballos

☑ **WORDS TO KNOW**
High-Frequency Words

are

now

Vocabulary Reader

How Many
Ducks?

Context Cards

The turtles are swimming.

COMMON CORE **RF.K.3c** read common high-frequency words by sight; **SL.K.2** confirm understanding of a text read aloud or information presented orally or through other media by asking/answering questions and requesting clarification

Go Digital

138

Words to Know

Read Together

▸ Read the words.

▸ Talk about the pictures.

are

1

The turtles **are** swimming.

now

2

The turtle is sleeping **now**.

Your Turn

Talk About It!

What animals can you find near a pond? Talk to a partner about it.

What Now?
by Suzanne Gerardi

Can Pam and Nan pat?
Nan can pat now.

Can Nat tap? Nat can!
Nat can tap now.

Sam and Bab are at bat.
Bat, Sam, bat!

Now we can nap, nap, nap.

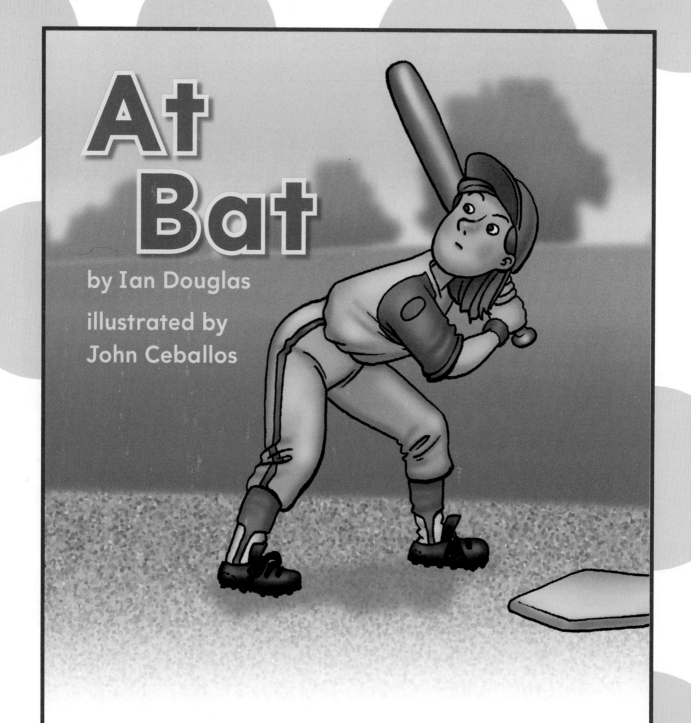

At Bat

by Ian Douglas

illustrated by

John Ceballos

See Bab at bat.

Bab can bat, bat, bat.

Bat now, Bab!
Bam!

See Pat.
Pat! Pat! Pat!

Pat! Pat! Pat! Pat!
We are ☺, Pat!

Pam Cat
by Nino Dimopolous
illustrated by Bari Weissmann

Come with Me
by Roger DiPaulo
illustrated by Fahimeh Amiri

☑ **WORDS TO KNOW**
High-Frequency Words

come

me

Vocabulary Reader

Context Cards

In the Sky
by Daniel Morgan

The rain will come down in spring.

COMMON CORE **RI.K.1** ask and answer questions about key details; **RI.K.2** identify the main topic and retell key details; **RF.K.3c** read common high-frequency words by sight

Go Digital

Words to Know

▶ You learned these words. Use each one in a sentence.

come

The rain will come down in spring.

me

This hat is for me.

Your Turn

Talk About It!

What can we see in the sky? Talk to a friend about it.

Pam Cat

by Nina Dimopolous

illustrated by Bari Weissmann

Mac sat and sat.

Pam Cat sat.

Mac can pat Pam Cat.

Pam Cat sat, sat, sat.
Mac can fan Pam Cat.

Pam, Pam, Pam!
Come to me, Pam Cat.

Come with Me

by Roger DiPaulo

illustrated by Fahimeh Amiri

Nat sat and sat.

Nat sat, sat, sat.

Come with me, Bab!
Bab! Bab! Bab!

Nat sat. Bab sat.

Nat can see Nan.

Bab can see Nan.

Nat sat. Bab sat. Nan sat.

Photo Credits

Placement Key: (r) right, (l) left, (c) center, (t) top, (b) bottom, (bg) background